OH·BOYZ!
THE NEW BOYZONE BOOK

Photographs by **Kyran O'Brien**

Words by **Aileen C O'Reilly**

All royalties to

Our Lady's Hospital for Sick Children, Dublin

THE O'BRIEN PRESS
DUBLIN

First published 1996 by
The O'Brien Press Ltd, 20 Victoria Road, Rathgar, Dublin 6, Ireland.

1 2 3 4 5 6 7 8 9 10
96 97 98 99 00 01 02 03 04 05

British Library Cataloguing-in-Publication Data
A catalogue reference for this title is available from the British Library

ISBN 0-86278-503-0

Typesetting, editing: The O'Brien Press Ltd.
Design: Frank Murphy
Colour separations: Lithoset Ltd.
Printing: Smurfit Web Press Ltd.

Kyran O'Brien wishes to thank the following companies for their support:

CONTENTS

"Right now we're just five young fellas having a good time. People can compare us to whoever they want but we're just five normal fellas who know that this will all end one day."
Mikey Graham,
June '96

Are *you* with the band?

It took a lot of laminates, endless notebooks, even more film and more than the occasional late night but we can now reveal the answers to lots of your questions ...

So why does Stephen gets hiccups just before he goes on stage? What exactly went on backstage in the hours leading up to the Boyz' first Wembley date? What is it really like being a pop idol *and* a dad? And who tends to cause havoc with his zany sense of humour every time there's serious work to be done? Prepare to find out more about the Boyz than you've ever thought possible — this is the one and only key to the life of those five Boyz from North Dublin. It's all here, the first access-all-areas account of a year in the life of Boyzone.

And what a crazy year it was. We found out exactly what Dublin's Fab Five got up to when they escaped the clutches of the camera and the music press — and here are the exclusive shots to prove it! We got up close and personal (when we finally battled our way through the Boyz' entourage of screaming fans) to experience the highs, the lows, the gruelling rehearsals, the photo shoots and the exhaustion on the road to Wembley with Ronan, Stephen, Keith, Shane and Mike. It's the Boyz' own story!

Aileen C O'Reilly and Kyran O'Brien

"Woooha! that's cold!"

can't get r...

7 UP

THE

Following in the well-worn footsteps of Take That, East 17 and New Kids On The Block – Shane has actually admitted to being a fan! – was a somewhat daunting task for the five good-looking boys from North Dublin back in '94. The era of the boy band had well and truly arrived and Take That were reigning supreme as the undisputed kings of the new movement. What chance did our Boyz have?

"They exuded this amazing enthusiasm from the word go," manager Louis Walsh remembers. "After being chosen from countless thousands and faced with the opportunity of being Ireland's first real boy band, they just lusted after the fame and success and the adoration. They saw the likes of Take That driving fans wild at the Point Depot in Dublin and they wanted that for themselves. I think that's definitely what got them through the early days when so many doors were shut in their faces and everyone laughed at the very idea of an Irish boy band.

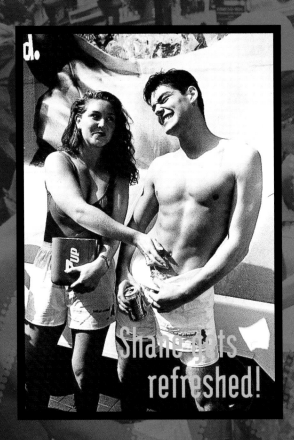

d.

Shane gets refreshed!

"Apart from that, there was precious little happening on the Irish pop scene at the time — if you could call it a pop scene, it had always been a rock tradition — so the timing was perfect."

"Let's face it, being plucked from obscurity and chosen out of thousands of other guys to be in a band is every kid's dream, isn't it?" Keith laughs. "I was so nervous but at the same time dead confident that we were going to be famous," he recalls. "It was a dream come true for me. I think we all believed right from the outset that suddenly anything was possible — and looking back at what we've achieved in the past couple of years just proves how right we were."

EARLY · DAYZ

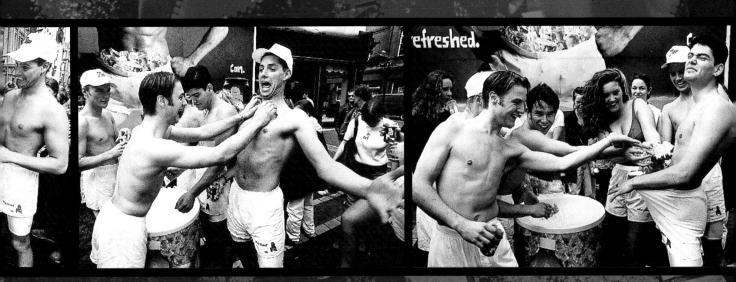

refreshed.

Bill Hughes – video supremo
– walking on air

Vennel making it work

"working my way
back to you, babe!"
'94

8

N A T I O N A L

Louis Walsh introduces
Ronan and Mikey to the media!

E N T E R T A I N M E N T A W A R D S

True recognition of Boyzone's arrival on the
music scene came in the form of their National
Entertainment Award in Dublin in December 1994.
After months of hard work they scooped the coveted
Best Irish Newcomers Award – an achievement
that doesn't come easily and put them on the list
of bands to be reckoned with. It was only a few
months since the Boyz had formed but the legions
of fans who'd been smitten by the five good-lookers
since they first warbled "Working My Way Back to

Phil Coulter and the Boyz

D E C E M B E R ' 9 4

the best newcomers '94

You, Babe" knew it was high-time
their idols were recognised as
serious talent. It was also perfect
timing – what better way to
start off your first nationwide
tour than with an award under
your belt!

ON THE RO

IRISH TOUR
SUMMER

From the relative ease of working in the studio and making an increasing number of personal appearances the Boyz launched into their first nationwide tour in July — a thirty-day blitz of every major city and town in Ireland. The "Unreal" tour, as it was christened, kicked off on 2 July 1995 at the Rialto in Derry in Northern Ireland and finally wound up on 31 July at the National Basketball Arena in Tallaght just outside Dublin — not surprisingly the entire tour was sold out well in advance.

Gruelling it most certainly was — but it was designed, as Louis Walsh confided, to leave the Boyz primed and in peak condition for their debut UK tour of twelve dates which was to follow immediately. "Yes, it was exhausting but it was necessary if they were going to be in with any chance of succeeding and breaking the UK market where the opposition is very tough. And, as I told them from the outset if they complained about being made to do this or that, if you want to be the best then you've got to put the work in — they used to hate me for that!"

"I never had any doubt about how much hard work we'd have to put in," Keith says, "but that tour nearly killed us! We didn't stop going between the time we started out at one end of the country and reached the other!"

Shane and Ronan say it with flowers

A D
' 9 5

RONAN KEATING

best buddy

We asked Ronan what it's like being one of the Boyz. "What can I say? I fully realise just how lucky I am. This is what we do and this is what we know — we don't know any better. And when you think about the sheer amount of physical hard work we have to put in — no, it's absolutely not easy and it is a very hard life. But it's knowing that it makes other people happy that makes it worthwhile for us. That's why I'm so proud to be in Boyzone. We're all so close. I tell you, some people are lucky to have two really good friends in their lives — I've got four of the best."

Was it difficult for the Boyz when Keith and Mike became dads — did it affect the band? "If anything, the lads grew up an awful lot when Keith and his girlfriend had Jordan and then Mike and his girlfriend had Hannah — but it hasn't changed the band in any way. We don't bring that into work.

"Right now Boyzone is our lives, it's what keeps us going. But the five of us don't even know what it is that makes us so special. We've never been anything other than ourselves — maybe that's the secret of our success!"

BOYZFILE
The low-down on Ronan

- **DATE OF BIRTH**
  3 March 1977

- **FAMILY**
  Three brothers, Gary, Gerard and Kieran and one sister, Linda

- **DISTINGUISHING FEATURE**
  The only self-confessed virgin in the band

- **BEST KNOWN FOR**
  Ronan has let it be known with no shadow of a doubt that he's proud to be a virgin and has no intention of doing anything about it until he meets Miss Right. Then, and only then, when he knows for sure that it is true love will there be any wedding bells. "Because I'm so romantic about all this, the time to make love has to be right. Of course I've been tempted but I want it to be special. So until then I'm not bothered."

- **PREVIOUS JOBS**
  You could have had this fine young thing at your feet and you mightn't even have known it — Ronan spent four years working part time in shoeshops!

- **MOST EMBARRASSING MOMENT**
  Innocent though he may look, don't let this boy deceive you. Ronan was constantly being sent out of class at school, leaving his teachers exasperated. In fact, despite his obviously angelic vocals, he was also asked to leave the school choir. "The teacher just kept not asking me back," he says, "so I got the hint after a while!"

- **BURNING AMBITION**
  To be a top singer/songwriter like Gary Barlow of Take That!

It was the night the world's jetset stepped out in Dublin draped in Irish designer gear. Eva Herzigova, Christy Turlington, Karen Mulder, Naomi Campbell and Jasmine Le Bon sashayed down the catwalk at the Point Depot for the hottest charity bash of the year.

The Brown

The Point

February

14

But the supermodels met their match when Stephen, Mikey, Keith, Ronan and Shane strutted into the limelight.

Daubed in body paint and sporting knitwear designer Lainey Keogh's finest, the boyz flexed their well-toned bods and then tore their designer threads to reveal tanned torsos. But the best was yet to come ...

Thomas Showcase of Irish Fashion Design

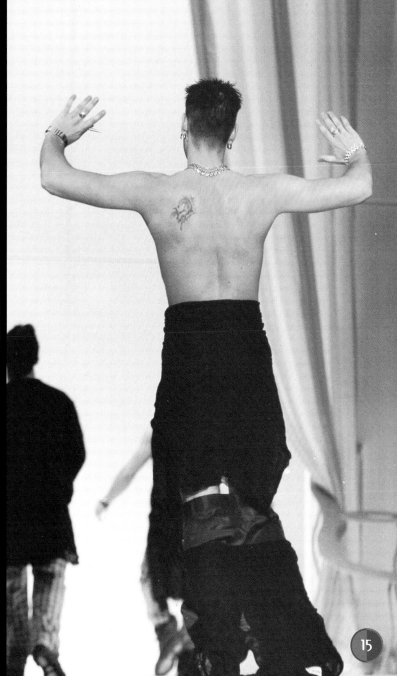

and then Shane dropped his trousers!

And the rest, as they say, is history. "That was just one of those things!" the stripper laughs, with more than a little wicked gleam in his eye. "Yeah, I know we said we'd never take our gear off, but we're still good clean guys behind it all. It was just a bit of fun."

'96

"It's funny though, 'cause we all knew we were gonna rip off the tops but I had it in the back of me mind when we got there that dropping the trousers might give us a bit of publicity. Anyway, I had to do *something* to match up to Naomi Campbell!"

And match up to Naomi Campbell and Co they most certainly did. The show marked a real coming of age for our Fab Five — not only were they out there at the ultimate glitzy bash of the year with the world's supermodels, but they also proved to anyone who might have doubted it before, that they were here, in your face and going to stay in the limelight right were they belonged!

Oh that rock-star chic!

"I'm actually very shy — but funnily enough, I love cameras. I feel alive when I'm playing to them. I loved every minute of the fashion show. Walking out there and hearing the whirr of the cameras and focusing in on just one, knowing that every photographer in the place is staring right at you just gives me such a rush. It's the best feeling."

Rehearsing for
the tour

The Summer Tour of '96 showed a whole new side to our Boyz' fancy footwork on the dancefloor. The routines were slicker and sexier than ever before — thanks to dance diva and choreographer to the stars Melinda McKenna and three weeks of intensive rehearsals, with time off for the odd photo shoot. We reckon all that practice made perfect though!

April '96

Recording

Phil Coulter

Boyzone's collaboration with the legendary Phil Coulter might not have seemed the obvious choice for a boy band but a glance at Mr Coulter's CV reveals that he's a veteran of the boy band scene — twenty years ago he worked closely with The Bay City Rollers who were Ireland's first-ever scream-inducing boy band — just ask your parents!

News that the chosen track was to be the traditional Irish air "She Moves through the Fair", also brought gasps of surprise from Boyzone fans. Hardly very rock 'n' roll, eh?

"She Moves through the Fair"

"At this stage, having achieved what they have achieved, I think the Boyz are sensible enough to know that success and stardom aren't God-given rights — if you want to be the best then you can never afford to stop working at it for a minute."

But, according to Phil, this was exactly why the Boyz had chosen the song. It was new and unexplored territory, and a good strong melody and lyrics that conjured up a mystical, Celtic feel was just what they were after. "I knew if we were going to do this then we had to do it properly — so I was seriously impressed with their eagerness to do something so off the wall."

hungry work!!

Phil describes the song. "It's a very dramatic arrangement and one that's destined to showcase the talents of the Boyz in a way that fans haven't seen before. That plus the fact that it's such a theatrical production should make a lot of people sit up and take notice."

Of all the Boyz Phil singles out Ronan for special mention. "It has to be said that Ronan has a lot of potential. I mean

I've worked with a lot of people down through the years, from big stars to less well-known ones and I was seriously impressed by this guy's ability and attitude. Apart from being a good singer, your focus and commitment are of paramount importance. You've got to be willing to take direction and be mature enough to know that you can learn a lot from others who know more than you."

But modest Ronan isn't interested in going solo or being the big boy of the band: "We're all equal in this band. I don't see myself as any frontman.

Steve grabs a quiet moment

does he ever stop eating?

My heart is in what I do and I never think much further down the line than that."

So how did that new all-Irish number go down? First to hear the song were those lucky Irish fans at the Point Depot in Dublin on 26 July. There was lots of nail-biting going on in the wings as all concerned waited with baited breath to see what would happen. Then, as the first haunting strains rang out, and the lasers scanned the ecstatic faces of the 8,000-strong crowd, everyone just knew ... This was like nothing Boyzone fans had ever heard from the band before — and they loved it!

Well done, Boyz!

Summer Tour '96

After months of gruelling preparation, rehearsing and fine-tuning, it was time to kick off the Summer Tour of '96 — the biggest tour of Boyzone's career to date. And the one that would see them surpass even their own wildest dreams.

Before they even stepped into the spotlight at their first gig in Rhyl in the UK at the end of April (chosen for the kick-off because it's quite a low-key venue), every single date was sold out.

According to Louis Walsh, it was phenomenal. "The new tour was leagues ahead of anything they'd ever attempted before. Apart from the fact that everything, including the venues, was on a larger scale, the Boyz were so much more polished this time round. I suppose it was all just so much sexier and raunchier and, looking back on it now, it was a real step up the ladder and something they worked relentlessly hard to achieve.

"They were determined from the outset that by the time they brought this tour back home to Dublin, it was going to be the best that it could be — creating the ultimate home-coming for their

last minute rehearsing

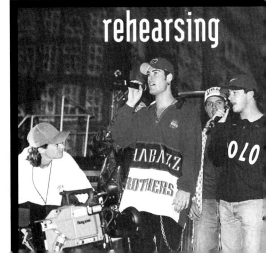

what *are* you talking about??

Irish fans was of paramount importance to them from the word go."

The Boyz began the second leg of their sell-out tour in Glasgow city on 5 July 1996 — and there was serious Boyzone mania in the air. So much so that Glasgow turned out to be one of the absolute highlights of the tour.

However, apart from all that last minute rehearsing which had to be endured (even though the Boyz could probably perform in their sleep at this stage!), and time out to talk to the hundreds of fans who were lucky enough to get into the "Meet and Greets", Stephen, Mike, Ronan and Keith took full advantage of Shane's regular snoozing sessions in his wardrobe (yes, he's known for this) and absconded with his skateboard. There's no better place for a skate than an empty stadium! Yes, despite those rigorous schedules you hear about, these Boyz always manage to find plenty of time for messing around backstage.

performing in their sleep?!

Steve and lookalike meet the fans

here's lookin' at you, babe

Shane snoozes in the wardrobe

Mikey shows off his skateboard skills

DID YOU KNOW?

On every night of every gig a large box of "top secret" goodies is delivered to the Boyz' dressing room — or all hell breaks loose.

Inside are 20 bottles of mineral water, 3 litres of orange juice, 12 cans of high-energy drinks, a selection of fresh fruit including plenty of bananas (apparently they're full of energy-giving stuff), a tray of dips and fresh vegetables, crisps, sweets and chocolate — but absolutely no alcohol. And that's just for starters — we got the Boyz' list of some of the things they just can't do without on tour (and exactly what they cost!)

- Hairgel £100
- Deodorant £120
- Honey and Lemon (for after-concert sore throats) £200

Launching

said and d

Chessingt
August

The guy behind all those fab videos, Bill Hughes, summed up the potential inherent in the Boyzone debut album when he remarked, "I think their greatest achievement to date has to be the fact that they wrote nine of the thirteen songs on

Said and Done. It instantly proved that they were here to stay for good — they weren't just a flash in the pan and I think their fans know this instinctively as well."

The scenes outside the Virgin Megastore in London's Oxford Street on 21 August 1995 said it all — forget the Blur v Oasis war, Boyzone toppled Albarn and the Gallagher clan out of the limelight when they arrived for a special public appearance on the day of their album launch and spent a hectic morning signing copies of *Said and Done.*

However, once they'd met the fans it was off to Chessington World of Adventures where the real partying was going on that night — typical of the Boyz to choose a theme park with some of the most serious "white knuckle rides" in the country for their launch! Especially since those of them who weren't in plaster were suffering from exhaustion!

Ronan with a shy fan

the Album

one

on

'95

The crowd appreciated, probably for the first time, exactly how tough it can be when you're a rock 'n' roll star. Shane was still on crutches after breaking his ankle while jumping off a wall in Sweden, Mikey was suffering from terrible neck pains, and Ronan's severe new haircut highlighted his gaunt features. Those designer shades were hiding serious luggage under the eyes. But the Boyz were determined to have a good time — even if they were fit to drop.

The most "happening" names on the London pop scene, including EYC, Gemini, Optimystic, Ultimate Kaos and Sean Maguire, turned

poor ol' Shane, he's broken his ankle!

up later on and roared their approval as the Boyz took to the specially constructed stage for a rousing rendition of "Key To My Life" — Shane, with his heavily plastered ankle, just about managed to stay upright, while the others leapt about and gave it their all.

Boyz at play —
tired but happy

However, war wounded or not, all five agreed that this was one night they had to end on the ultimate high — on the famous Rameses Revenge ride.

hold on tight, Boyz!

Stephen, Shane, Mikey, Ronan and Keith bundled in — only to be joined by the rest of the party crew (in their best clobber!). Things were getting seriously out of hand, Sean Maguire was looking decidedly uneasy and every one of the Ultimate Kaos boys looked positively pale ...

Yeeeaarrrgggghhhh! A blood-curdling scream went up as the gigantic arms swung into action and hurled the future of pop (and their manager's blood pressure) hurtling high into the night sky before being submerged in the icy waters below.

anyone fancy a swim?

On and on it went until everyone begged to be released. Eventually the worn-out party staggered back to *terra firma* and the celebrations continued well into the night before the Boyz were whisked away in the wee hours.

Think how soundly they would have slept if they'd known then that they had a No. 1 smash-hit debut album on their hands!

JULY 7th-8th

Keith gets ready for the stage!

Next stop on the tour was Birmingham and the Boyzone mothership took over the NEC, causing all-out mania at the first sight of the Boyz in their red PVC. Every gig at this stage was conquering new territory — territory which before would have belonged exclusively to Take That. However, judging from the reaction the Boyz got, which grew more and more intense every night, Boyzone fans appreciate a good thing when they see it ...

Of course, it wasn't just the Boyz performing their funked-up dance routines and swoon-laden lyrics that caused such a stir — their new look was also raising more than a few eyebrows.

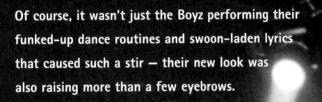

Alex Delves was the man responsible for redesigning Boyzone's seriously raunchy onstage wardrobe for the new tour. Gone were the old firemen's outfits and the gangster clobber and in their place were designer gauze shirts, muscle tops, red PVC

combats and full-length leather coats — suffice it to say, if temperatures weren't already dangerously high, they soon went soaring through the roof!

And, apart from the impact that the new "raunch factor"

...was having, a new star was emerging in the group. For the first time Stephen was getting a shot at performing solo and everyone concerned suddenly realised that another talent in Boyzone had been tapped.

Steve has always given the shows his all. "The stage is very important to me," he says. "All these people who come to see our shows, they've paid to see us, they're there for us and it's up to us to give them the best show we possibly can.

"When I'm up there I'll single out a girl in the audience and try to make eye contact. When I do, I'll wink and smile at her and I feel just great when she beams back and she's delighted. It's strange, but brilliant, to know that you make people happy by just doing something you enjoy."

His solo rendition of "If You Were Mine" (complete with his unashamed knack of playing up to the cameras and staring out in a dreamy daze) left the NEC in a state of emotional turmoil — which didn't lessen when the rest of the band returned onstage in yet more new gear ...

STEPHEN GATELY

caring
sharing
romantic

What's been happening with Steve since the Boyz took off? We asked him how life had changed for him. "Looking back over everything that's happened over the past two years I think the most important achievement for me personally has definitely been the fact that all this has made me so much more aware of what's going on in my life and in the world. I suppose I have matured (gulp!) a lot as a result but I'm still the same old Stevie underneath.

"That said, I'm not Mr Happiness all the time. Things get to me just like anyone else and I have my off days. Usually when I can't get any time to myself or some semblance of a private life. That is something that I still find very hard to cope with.

"I don't conform to this theory that you naturally outgrow those people you grew up with and if your life changes for the better then you've instantly nothing in common with them anymore. My friends and my family still play a very important role in my life. My parents in particular are still very special to me — maybe that's because I'm a homeboy at heart and I get homesick very easily!

"Ronan, Shane, Keith and Mike are my four best mates but it's still really important to me that I get home to see my parents regularly so I can just hang out and do normal things like making the tea and going down to the shop for my mam — I'm serious!

"It's funny thinking about it, but if I hadn't been picked for the band then I'd still have ended up on the stage anyway since I was always big into acting. It's something that makes you a lot more confident and anyone who suffers from shyness should do it — believe me!"

B O Y Z F I L E
The low-down on Steve

- **DATE OF BIRTH**
  17 March, St Patrick's Day, 1976

- **FAMILY**
  Three brothers, Mark, Tony and Alan and an older sister, Michelle

- **DISTINGUISHING FEATURE**
  A tattoo of a Tasmanian Devil on his hip

- **BEST KNOWN FOR**
  Claiming he's never been in love — oh, and those dreamy blue eyes and that dangerously cute smile

- **PREVIOUS JOBS**
  Steve was a familiar figure in Makullas on Suffolk Street for some time before fame came knocking. However, he also spent some time scrubbing glasses at a theatre and even strutting his stuff on the catwalk before becoming a star

- **MOST EMBARRASSING MOMENT**
  Unfortunately, Steve is something of a goodie-goodie when it comes to bad behaviour. The only time he can remember getting into trouble is when he was in French class. Apparently the poor boy was so smitten with the *mademoiselle* teaching him the language of *lurve* that he couldn't concentrate on his work at all!

- **BURNING AMBITION**
  To sing on a Disney blockbuster sound track and have a house overlooking Killiney beach in Dublin

way...

If there was ever even the tiniest doubt that Boyzone mania existed outside Ireland and the UK then the Summer '96 trip to Paris certainly proved otherwise — as the French contingent of star-struck fans who kept a non-stop vigil outside the swish Le Parc Hotel would agree.

After a blitz of photo shoots and radio interviews the Boyz were whisked off to appear on two of France's top-rating TV shows. First up

THE HIT MACH

PARIS '96

"Love me for a reason"

was "The Hit Machine", the French equivalent of "Top of the Pops". This prestigious (and crazy!) show features the cream of European pop, performing before a few hundred screaming fans with more than a few interesting capers going on between the presenters and their guests. This time round Boyzone were going in front of the cameras. A quick visit to make-up and, with no idea what was in store for them, the Boyz stepped out ...

Some lucky Boyzone fans had won the chance to meet their idols in the flesh, but that wasn't all. They also got to sing a tribute to the five blushing lads before being presented with their very own Boyzone dolls. The Boyz stood by as the smitten French ladies sang their way through

...hey!

a quick touch-up before going on!

I N E

"Love Me for a Reason" — every single word delivered with heart-felt devotion. The Boyz then returned the favour and sang the song right back, before Ronan took the lead and launched into "Father & Son", which was in danger of becoming a new French national anthem!

their very own toy Boyz!

C'mon, everybody!

22

PARIS
THE DANCE

it was this big!

did I tell you
the one about...

40

23   23A   24   24A   25   25A   26   26A

'96
MACHINE

Straight after "The Hit Machine", with hardly
a second to comb their locks and straighten
their designer clobber, the Boyz were off to
record "The Dance Machine" along with their
miniature lookalikes — the Boyzone dolls.

The Dance Machine was a massive televised
gig with a live screamadelic audience of
15,000. Again, the guys sent pulses soaring into overdrive
with heart-wrenching renditions of "Love Me for a Reason"
and "Father & Son" which they performed in the company
of top all-singing all-dancing acts
such as Worlds Apart, Backstreet
Boys, Coronas and PJ & Duncan.

shane sings to his fans

MIKE GRAHAM

deep sensitive *poet*

Did Mikey ever dream that he might be a megastar one day? "I just always knew that my life was heading in this direction. Something in me always knew that this is what it was heading towards. I don't know, ask the others, I've always had this really great faith in my destiny."

But it's not as if this makes being a star easy. "I can honestly say I've never worked so hard, both mentally and physically. It's very intense to say the least — the fact that I'm not a 'morning person' doesn't exactly help either."

Has he changed since Boyzone hit the big-time? "What has changed is my motivation — that's what my daughter Hannah is now and it's knowing that I'm doing all this for her that gets me out of bed in the morning. She's my reason for wanting all this success — I want to be the best for her.

"I think her arrival instantly put a focus on the band for me rather than distracting me from it. I may have been a bit wild but now I know I've got a little person to care for who relies on me for everything and looks up to me. That's the most amazing feeling — and it makes you realise pretty quickly that there's far more to life than the single lifestyle."

BOYZFILE
The low-down on Mike

- **DATE OF BIRTH**
  15 August 1972

- **FAMILY**
  Five sisters, Yvonne, Avril, Kathy, Claire and Debbie and one brother, Niall

- **DISTINGUISHING FEATURE**
  A great Elvis impersonation

- **BEST KNOWN FOR**
  Being the "deep" and serious one in the band and for needing space and time to himself when the band are on tour

- **PREVIOUS JOBS**
  Another mechanic in the making — but fortunately for us Mikey realised he didn't want to hide his vocal ability and good looks underneath a stream of spluttering engines for the rest of his days

- **MOST EMBARRASSING MOMENT**
  Somehow we're sure that every Boyzone fan is well-aquainted with Mikey's most embarrassing moment. It involved a horse and Mikey's leg which got stuck in a stirrup. Our young horseman lost his balance on his trusty steed but his foot remained stuck fast in the stirrup. Meanwhile his charge ran across the fields. Oouch! "I thought that was the end," he now laughs looking back on it all. "That horse just seemed to drag me on forever — it was terrifying!"

- **BURNING AMBITION**
  To be a good father to daughter Hannah and write hit songs

JULY 13th

reaching for the top

flying high!

Keith hits a high note

Under the sweltering heat of the July sun, Boyzone launched their attack on Wembley arena — not once, not twice, not even three times but an astounding four times and each one a *fan*tastic sell-out gig. They played on the weekend of 13 and 14 July and then returned to Wembley for the grand finale to their UK tour on the 30 and 31 July.

"It's mad!" Louis Walsh said. "I mean I always believed we'd do one Wembley gig — but four sell-out gigs? It's crazy and it's so brilliant!" It was the culmination of over two years of relentless hard work and of sheer dogged determination to succeed where the cynics had scoffed that they were bound to fail.

arta Boyz!

"cute – what me?"

Ronan puts his best foot forward

On Saturday 13 July the fab five leapt out of the cage that appeared centre-stage in a smoke haze of dry-ice to the thundering bass-lines of "Together". Boyzone had claimed the throne of popdom and the screams told it all. The long wait was over for the lucky 24,000 fans who would see the Boyz that weekend.

From the moment that the intro to "Together" first ripped through the audience to the last strains of "Different Beat" (which was originally to have been the new single) their performance shone with the polish of a professional act.

Thanks to the rigorous coaching of Melinda McKenna, every move was timed with split-second precision and the show had been injected with a serious raunch factor.

Ronan held court centre-stage while Stephen, Mike, Shane and Keith made full use of the set — putting all that coaching into action. The crowd didn't know where to look as images of each of the Boyz flashed up on the large screens that hung on either side of the stage.

Ah yes, and those awkward costume changes had been dealt with as well. Instead of waiting for the Boyz to

thumbs up, Boyz!

re-emerge dressed in more fab gear, the crowd never lost sight of their idols — this time round an agile cameraman raced backstage with them to their dressing-room and showed fans exactly what a zoom lens can do ...

Unfortunately though, heavy PVC doesn't go too well with July weather — the Boyz were drenched in sweat before they'd even plunged into the second verse of "Together" and there was no sign of things cooling down. All of London was frying in the searing heatwave. "It's all thanks to you, our wonderful fans, that we're here tonight," a sweat-drenched, emotional Mikey yelled at 12,000 roaring fans. "We'd never have made it without your support."

high-ee ya!

rhapsody in blue

JULY 14th

what a deadly duo!!

After the second sell-out Wembley date, on Sunday 14 July, the Boyz had a chance to relax and chat backstage. (They took off instantly after their first date in Ronan's black BMW with most of their backing band's gear!) On stage that night they had looked every inch the superstars as their silver jackets sent splintering shards of light in every direction. It was the glittering highlight of a meteoric rise to pop superstardom for five guys who'd had beer glasses, not fluffy toys, flung at them when they had first set out only two and a half years before.

fans get a quick glimpse!

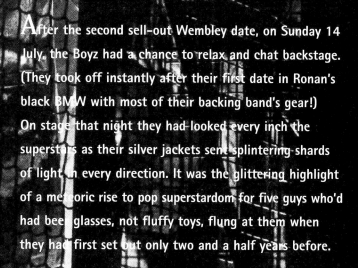

Steve struts his stuff

49

Steve belts it out!

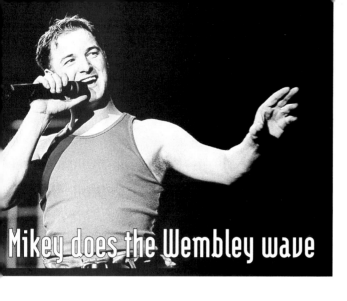

Mikey does the Wembley wave

"You know when you get to play Wembley Arena that you've really arrived," Ronan said, laughing. "It's not that it's the biggest gig going or anything, but you just know you must be doin' all right when you get it."

Keith remarked: "Now, of course, we accept all the adulation those same people fling at us — after all, at the end of the day, we're the ones that are coming out on top, and it's very much a case of who's laughing now, isn't it? This is the dream." As Ronan made clear later it was obvious that the Boyz had surpassed even their own expectations. "I sat on that stage singing 'Father & Son' and for the first time I took out my monitor and heard them all singing every word back to me," he admitted later. "It brought more than a tear to my eye, I can tell you. I mean I remember our first gig when there were no more than twenty people there — and now this?!"

The Boyz made no secret of the fact that the two nights at the Point Depot in Dublin were going to be, in their eyes, the ultimate gigs of the tour. But as far as the Irish fans were concerned when they read about the concert in the British papers and heard about their idols taking Wembley by storm, they knew the Boyz had reached the top.

Stephen beamed when he said, "I can't wait to take this show back home to everyone in the Point — that'll be really special. I'm sorry, this is just all so unbelievable. If I think about it anymore I'll go mad — I've got butterflies about Dublin already and we're not even there yet!"

fans sing back to Ronan

Steve sitting pretty with Ruby and Dani!

THE IRMA AWARDS

Congratz, Boyz!

From Van the Man and Joe Elliot to Dani Behr and Ruby Wax, the music fraternity joined the glitterati and traded in their leathers and denims for *haute couture* and tuxedos on 29 March 1996 for the slickest music bash of the year — the IRMA Awards.

For the Boyz, just back from a gruelling stint in the Far East, the news that they'd scooped two awards — the Best Irish Band Award and the Best Single Award for "Key To My Life" — to add to their '95 award for Best New Band, was the perfect welcome home.

THE BURLINGTON
DUBLIN '96

Outside the Burlington Hotel in Dublin hordes of dedicated Boyzone fans set up camp in the hopes of catching a glimpse of their heroes.

Inside, the cream of the UK and the Irish music industry mingled under swirling psychedelic lights until the small hours of the morning as the champagne continued to flow. When the organisers did their sums later they found the event had raised £25,000 for charity.

Wild child, ex-"The Word" presenter and hostess of "Hotel Babylon", Dani Behr, did the honours by presenting Boyzone with the Best Band Award — they returned the honour five times over by surrounding her for the entire evening and ensuring nobody else got a word in edgeways!

Ex-Eternal girl, Louise Nurding, also dropped in to wish the Boyz well, as did ex-"Eastenders" girl, Michelle Gayle. It didn't take long before the Boyz and girls were deep in conversation and oblivious to the celebrating going on around them, not to mention the focus of all those zoom lenses.

However, the Boyz' feathers were more than a little ruffled when the band didn't pick up their second award for Best Single. Apparently the organisers simply forgot about it!

Mikey has a quick pose with Therapy?

Michelle Gayle puts a smile on Mikey's face!

Steve sitting it out with Ruby!

Ronan wasn't too impressed by the oversight. "I had my acceptance speech prepared an' all — I was really looking forward to it. But it was great to get the Best Irish Band Award ... It's great to come home to this."

It was also the night when Louis Walsh put paid to all the rumours regarding Keith's impending marriage to pregnant girlfriend Lisa Smith. Those hoping to hear the sound of wedding bells were told they'd be waiting for a long time. "It's definitely not going to happen," he said. "Keith is not getting married, absolutely not. His career comes first."

But it was the news of the awards that really stole the show. "We were absolutely delighted to get the two awards," Louis Walsh said, "especially since we won the Best New Band Award last year. It's brilliant for the Boyz, a real acknowledgement of what they've achieved to date."

"As for fame and fortune and all that — well, we had hopes and dreams but we never imagined that it would all happen quite so fast. What can I say? We constantly have to try and keep our feet on the ground — even though we still intend to be the biggest band in the world." Ronan '96

And so Boyzone descended on the King's Hall in Belfast in Northern Ireland, a rather larger venue than they had played only twelve months before. The last time round it was the Ulster Hall that was rocked to its foundations during the band's nationwide Summer Tour of '95.

JULY 24th

The King's Hall, on the other hand, was worlds apart — the fans knew it and the Boyz were relishing every moment of their soaring super-stardom. Keeping those feet on the ground was going to be a tough task, judging by the reception that greeted them that night.

At that stage, of course, speculation was building, in the wake of Robbie Williams's break from Take That that Ronan was being groomed as the new Gary Barlow (while Gary was off trying to become the new Elton John!). But it didn't take long for "Tin-Tin" — the nickname was inspired by that spiky bonce Ronan was sporting for a while — to put everyone straight on the matter. Not interested, he said.

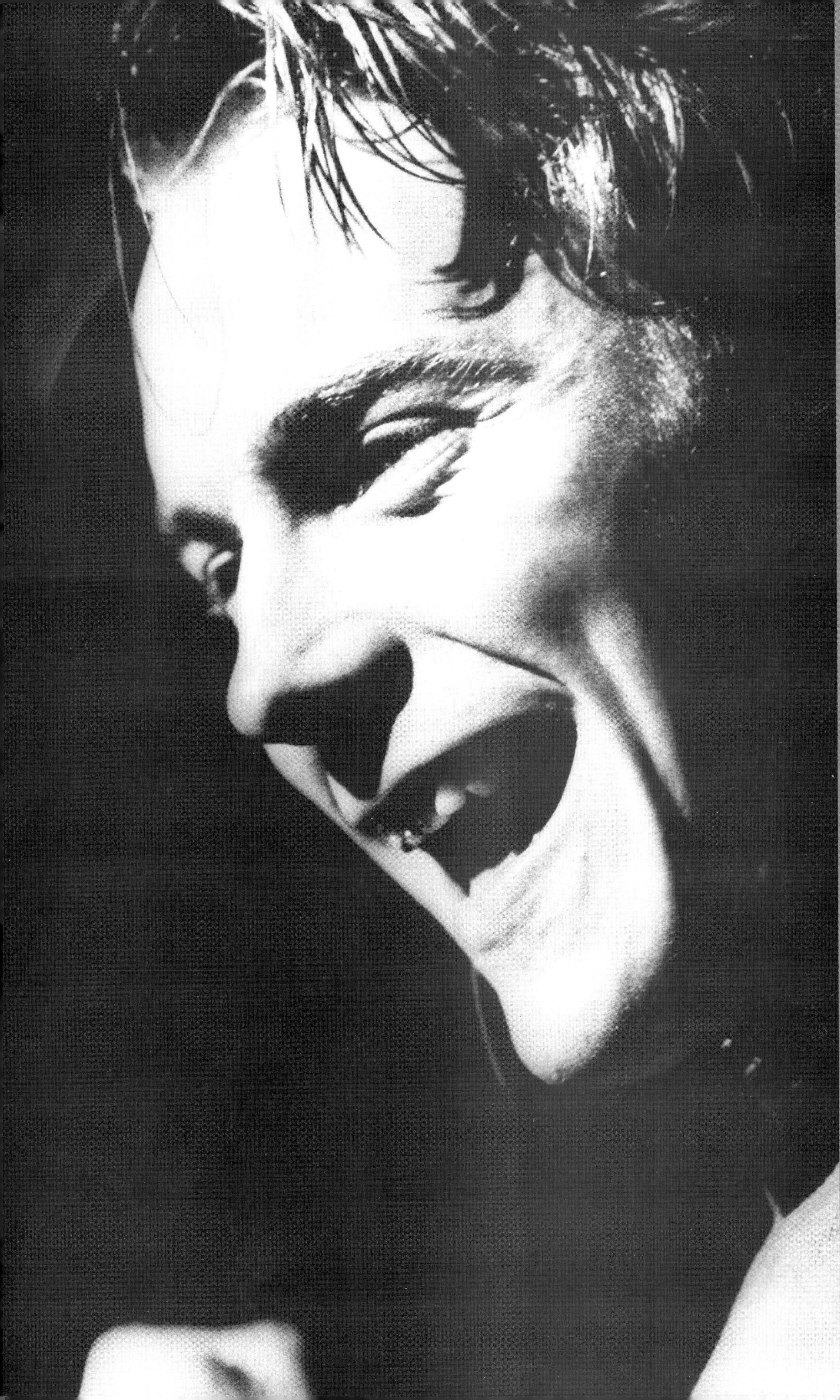

belfast '96

He and the Boyz were totally dedicated to Boyzone. "Right now, Boyzone is our lives — and it's what keeps us going. It isn't a nine-to-five for us in any respect. We don't get home after a hard day's night. People assume we go to all these wild parties every night after we come off stage, but you're so wrecked after a gig that you just want to crawl back to your hotel bedroom and sleep."

The Boyz certainly weren't entertaining the prospect of any chic bashes that night and, true to their word, all five hit the sack ASAP once they had said their goodbyes to the fans at the King's Hall.

Not that they had much choice in the matter — a privately chartered 18-seater jet was taking them straight to Denmark at a crazy hour the next morning. There they would perform a huge open-air gig before returning to Dublin to take on the Point Depot ...

OUT · AND

MAIN STREET, U.S.A.
DISNEYLAND PARIS

the Boyz
visit Eurodisney

where's my lunch?

P A

Steve gives a French fan a quick hug!

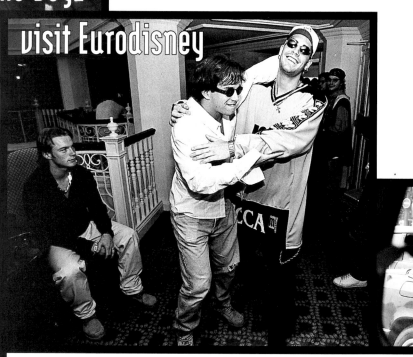

ABOUT · IN

When in the city of the chic, do what the natives do — POSE!!! And don't those bare chests say it all, eh? Once they hit the blazing June sunshine in the City of Lights the Boyz took an executive decision and left their schedules locked in the boot of the car — for one afternoon at least! Keep your Louvre and your Champs Elysee, Paris had just acquired its most alluring tourist attraction ... The fact that all five Boyz were as fascinated with Paris as it was with them meant it was time for some serious sightseeing and a well-earned bout of sun-worshipping — and if they happened to bump into some *mademoiselles* along the way then all the better!

RIS

Their rather obvious VIP set of wheels and tinted glass windows were given the heave-ho and the real sightseeing began. As you can see from these shots, the Eiffel Tower was a suitable setting for some serious leg work. Of course, it became all too much for Keith who took a leaf from Shane's book and decided to grab some shut-eye in the middle of the road (please don't try this at home unless you fancy having permanent track marks down your front!).

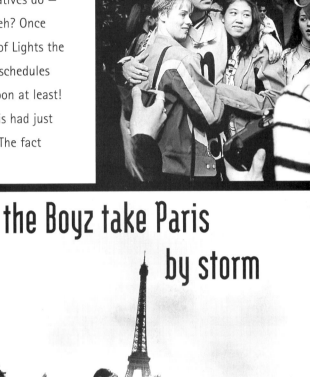

the Boyz take Paris by storm

Mikey has a quick trim

gotcha! Shane and future
Boyzone member Conal

Shane performs offstage too!

Oh, what will I have?

Life backstage on the Summer Tour of '96 was well-orchestrated chaos and as hectic as any two hour performance the Boyz put in onstage — except you never quite knew what was going to happen next, especially as those Boyz have a tendency to get ever so slightly restless ...

One very special VIP dropped in at Wembley and demanded the Boyz' full and undivided attention all evening — well, he did offer them all of his jelly babies as a bribe. Who could possibly command such attention? Conal, Ronan's nephew, was the show-stealer — backstage at least. Rumour has it he's shaping up very well as a potential sixth member of the band.

BOYZ·AT·PLAY

anyone fancy a sandwich?

Ronan cools down
after jogging

Is that *me* ?!

The hours just before a show are sacrosanct for the
Boyz. It's that special time when the really hard work
is put in, like eating vast amounts of nosh, hosing
down after that jog — yes, that is Ronan the Fireman
— or scaring your crew a whiter shade of pale by
disappearing on the nearest vintage motorbike. Mikey,
will you please step forward and explain yourself?

Yes indeed, he may be the oldest member of the
band — twenty-four and a daddy into the bargain —
but once Mikey spied the bike, he couldn't resist the

Mikey ´n´ friend
take a spin

urge to get it running and out on the highway (well, he didn't quite make it out of the gates). With friend in tow, he gave the machine the test drive of its life — to a chorus of cheering from the fans outside the gates who were clamouring for a better view.

And Shane decided to get his own back on Melinda McKenna (the Boyz' funky new choreographer who dreamt up all those exhausting but raunchy routines for the Summer Tour of '96) by teaching her to skateboard — with a little help from Mikey. But, as these pictures show, one skateboard between three people isn't the best way of teaching — or learning. Whoops! Mind that wall!

With all this kamikaze-style action going on, the crew was greatly relieved when the Boyz finally decided to swap their "outdoor pursuits" for a spell in front of the telly during Euro '96. At least their charges wouldn't get up to too much mischief when the footie kicked in ...

Mikey, Shane 'n' Melinda go overboard!

Keith reveals his fav team!

the Boyz catch up on Euro '96

KEITH DUFFY

soul boy

All that fame, how has it affected our Soul Boy — is he the same Keith that he used to be? "I'm definitely not the same person on stage — when I'm up there I'm totally psyched out, a superstar popstar performing for my wonderful fans — but, no, I don't think fame has changed me. I still believe that the best things in life are free and that's what I intend to pass on to Jordan. I intend to be an ordinary dad — it doesn't matter what my job is now or how I earn my money."

So, does this mean we won't be seeing the next generation of the Duffy clan on "Top of the Pops" in the years to come? "No, I wouldn't say that at all. I mean, even knowing what I've gone through to get where I am now, even that would never make me discourage Jordan from getting involved in this business. I wouldn't discourage him in anything he wanted to do. I have no influence over what he wants — just like my little brother John, who's getting a band together at the moment.

"My mam has seen what I've gone through from day one but she still wouldn't discourage John from doing anything he'd set his heart on. She lost me for a long time to the band with the touring and everything but she'd still back John up if that was what he wanted."

So what does Keith think of his own band's music? "I do actually quite like Boyzone's music — especially the new album *A Different Beat*. It's absolutely brilliant and it's going to be No. 1 all over the world. It's not that it's a major step forward for the band, but it does show that we're definitely moving on. We're received an awful lot of respect now — other boy bands starting out now are looking up to us. It's as if we've been crowned."

BOYZFILE
The low-down on Keith

- **DATE OF BIRTH**
  1 October 1974

- **FAMILY**
  Two brothers, Derek and John

- **DISTINGUISHING FEATURE**
  Short-sighted but still refuses to wear glasses

- **BEST KNOWN FOR**
  Being the hell-raiser in the band — and for becoming the first dad!

- **PREVIOUS JOBS**
  Keith had designs on a career as an architect but chucked it in when he set his heart on the showbiz lifestyle — he ended up as a strip-o-gram! However, his raunchy dancing stood to him when he went to audition for the band and the rest, as they say, is history

- **MOST EMBARRASSING MOMENT**
  Well, let's say he didn't take too kindly to over enthusiastic snappers trying to grab a shot of girlfriend Lisa and baby Jordan at Dublin Airport. He let them know in no uncertain terms that it's only polite to ask first and snap later if and when you get daddy's approval!

- **BURNING AMBITION**
  To be happy, healthy, rich and famous and the best "New Age" dad on the block

JULY

It was an exhausted Ronan, Stephen, Mikey, Shane and Keith who jetted into Dublin late on the night of 25 July 1996 after barely touching down in Denmark the day before. At this stage the Boyz were beginning to feel they were spending more time in the air than on the ground (whatever country that happened to be). Only the day before that they had been playing in Belfast. But an unforeseen glitch in their touring schedule meant that their Denmark concert fell between the Belfast and the Dublin dates. So much for the jetsetting lifestyle, eh?

The chartered jet took the Boyz to Odense in Denmark early on 25 July where they played to a crowd of 15,000 Danish fans in blistering heat at the prestigious outdoor Langelands Festival. Coincidentally, fellow Irish band the Corrs also headlined there that weekend.

And once they set foot in the Danish countryside there wasn't time — even for Shane who, of course, can sleep standing up — to catch any shut-eye.

Keith and Ronan give it all they've got

"We're just five young fellas havin' a good time. People can compare us to whoever they want — but it doesn't change the fact that we're just five normal fellas who know that this will all end one day." Mikey '96

25th

denmark '96

"I think I can honestly say," Mikey added later on, "that I've never worked so hard, both mentally and physically, as I have on this tour. It's been very intense, to say the least. But whether or not you stay the pace is very much your own decision — no one wants to be under constant strain. Right now though, all we're concerned with is being as successful as we possibly can!"

Of course, it's hard to believe the dream could ever end when you see the Boyz in action. Apart from all the strutting and dreamy-eyed looks on stage there's

"There's just something about doing a huge outdoor festival like that — the sun's beating down, the crowd's going wild and even the fact that you're in a foreign country where people don't speak your language, even that doesn't lessen the whole atmosphere — it's amazing. Especially when you realise how much you mean to these people, people you've never seen before but they've followed everything you've every done. It's a brilliant feeling — I get butterflies just thinking about it."

no shortage of laughing and kid-acting going on — and they're not averse to the odd group hug depending on how emotional they're feeling at the time and how close to collapse!

"I've seen bands and the only time they're together is when they're on stage," Shane explained when we asked him did he ever feel that they were being forced to live in each other's pockets — especially on tour. "Some bands even have separate dressing-rooms. It's like for them being in the band is just a business — or some professional thing they do for a living. We, on the other hand, seriously enjoy being with each other. It's what keeps us going."

JULY 26th-28th

Dublin welcomed her Boyz home with all the feeling of a mother re-united with her long-lost sons. By the time the private jet landed in Dublin Airport late on 25 July, there was more than a touch of hysteria in the air. And, although there was no doubt that Wembley Arena was the jewel in the

the Boyz introduce

dancers for the first time

crown of their UK tour, Dublin held an extra-special place in our Boyz' hearts. Eight thousand fans were just about to learn how special ...

"This time round we weren't going to play Ireland unless we had our full Summer Tour of '96 production," Shane explained.

"We just refused to do it without the set we'd been using throughout the UK tour. It's crazy, we've never been able to give Dublin audiences the 'real' Boyzone gig we've been working so hard to perfect."

"What can I say, Dublin? It's so good to be home!" Ronan yelled with tears in his eyes when the cry of "We love you, Boyzone!" went up. "There's a real feeling of pride for us being here tonight," said Mike. "That and the fact that we're finally getting the chance to show everyone, especially our faithful fans, exactly what Boyzone are capable of."

Shane was doing quite a good job of that himself. As the undoubted sex symbol of the troop, he played up to the cameras at every opportunity — his newly extended locks upping the oomph! factor considerably.

But it was Stephen who hijacked every heart in the vicinity with his rendition of "If You Were Mine". "That was the most amazing gig," he said afterwards. "Did you see the way they went wild out there? I'd been dreaming about this for so long that once I got out there I didn't want to ever come down off that stage. To finally come home to Dublin and be able to give our fans a show like this — it was such a rush."

SHANE LYNCH

Mr ultra cool

It's not easy getting a moment to yourself if you're a megastar, according to Shane. "If you're worried about keeping your private life private then this is the wrong business to be in. If you try to hide something from the press then they'll just go ahead and write it anyway. Whereas, if you just get on with it and don't make out like you're hiding anything, then they won't give a toss about you. It's when you try to have a private life that the trouble starts."

But there are compensations ... "This, a tough life? No way! I completely enjoy what I do — it's not a hard life to live at all. We didn't know that things were ever going to get this big. That said, we never contemplated a downfall — from day one we were always so positive about this even though it was never easy with all the opposition we had. It was all hope and 'please God, it'll work out,' from the word go."

Even so, it wasn't always smooth going. Has the struggle changed Shane? "No, despite everything that's happened

to me in the past two years I honestly don't think I've changed that much. Certain things have, of course, but not the important things — not me as a person. The trouble is, in this business, people don't have to know you to categorise you. It's like forming opinions is a kind of knee-jerk reaction — it's really bad."

BOYZFILE
The low-down on Shane

- **DATE OF BIRTH**
  1 July 1976

- **FAMILY**
  Five sisters, Catherine, Keavy, Adele, Alison and Tara

- **DISTINGUISHING FEATURE**
  That interesting eyebrow!

- **BEST KNOWN FOR**
  Being a dedicated follower of fashion — he's as much at home in the front row of a fashion show as he is onstage. He takes his image very seriously and his favourite designers include Versace, Armani, Calvin Klein, and D & G — just for starters!

- **PREVIOUS JOBS**
  No doubt the number of female teenage drivers on the road would have doubled if Shane had decided to stick at being a car mechanic for the rest of his life. Somehow though, we think he would have been wasted down there under the bonnet ...

- **MOST EMBARRASSING MOMENT**
  Those shots of him at the Boyzone album launch in Chessington say it all! The poor hobbling popstar got a terrible slagging from the rest of the Boyz as he tried to limp around on crutches and keep his ultra cool image. By all accounts his clumsiness was legendary ...

- **BURNING AMBITION**
  Just to be happy — so he says!

Keith proves that burnt toast is very nutritious.

"Look, I hate yellow flowers okay?"

Take one more picture of me and I'm phoning my lawyer!

B O Y Z B

This man's been following us around for months now, any idea who he is...?

Look into my eyes, you are feeling sleepy...

Ooh! I definitely should *not* have had that second veggie burger!

Ronan taking a shower al fresco — this man has an obsession with water!

Y·BOYZ

Steve, that aftershave is dreadful!

Excuse me, do I know you?

Sean Maguire, Ronan and mysterious smiling friend.

Hey, its a tough job — what can I say?

Feeling the chill, Steve?

Hello, 'ello, 'ello!

I'm goin' nowhere until I get my dessert!

"Look mam, I promise I'm in bed at 9.00pm every night, honest."

I could have been a model, you know.

Look, no hands.

My smile is bigger than your's!

Shane, I think we're really lost this time!

The Boyz are so used to being tailed by photographers everywhere they go that they're sure there's nothing to this camera snapping malarky — all you have to do is point and press, right? Anyone can do that ...

So after numerous promises from Stephen that he's an "accomplished" photographer (and the one band member who'd definitely get us those "interesting" shots of the Boyz caught unawares), we let all five of the Boyz loose with some cameras — just to see what they would come up with. The end result, as you can see from these pages, may not be exactly what David Bailey or Herb Ritts would be after, but we reckon a career behind the lens might not be out of the question if the Boyz get fed up with fame and fortune. After all, the face-pulling alone in this snapshot collection (Ronan, what were you looking at?) makes it worthwhile. They even stole a pic of ace-photographer Kyran himself ...

Boyz on Screen

These days the Boyz look just at home on screen as they do on stage. It's all a long way from that very first timid appearance on "The Late, Late Show", Ireland's most popular TV chatshow, back in '94 when the Boyz didn't even know each other's names, let alone the fact that in a few short months they'd be national heroes. It was, as Shane admitted, "the gig that nearly killed us before we even got started!"

It's a different story now — as you can see from these pix of the Boyz enjoying themselves onstage — and backstage — at the "Kelly Show Special". Also along that night were "Lord of the Dance" himself, Michael Flatley, and comedian Tom O'Connor — so laughs were guaranteed. Looking tanned,

relaxed and successful in their white designer shirts (especially Ronan in that light-white number!), the Boyz performed "Father & Son" and "Love Me for a Reason" to wild applause, before they kicked back and chatted with Gerry Kelly about life in the "Oh! Zone".

there'll be none of that, Louis!

everyone smile for the camera!

hup-ya...

Of course, within minutes of the Boyz' arrival, all hell broke loose outside the venue in Belfast where the show was being recorded live. Once the 200 fans fortunate enough to get their hands on tickets had been let in, reinforcements from the police had to be called in to "babysit" the crowd outside!

Who knows where those Boyz will get to next — though, if Steve has anything to do with it, they'll be off to Disneyland to record the soundtrack for a Big Screen cartoon classic!

...oops!

very funny, Tom!

RONAN'S
birthday bash

happy birthday, son!

One of the highlights of 1996 for Ronan had to be his nineteenth birthday back in March — and we went along to the party to snap the birthday boy. Where was it held? Well, that was classified information at the time. Rumour had it that the Boyz had decided to head off to a secret location in London instead of risking scenes like those at HMV in Dublin's Grafton Street (6,000 fans turned up to see their idols and the police had to be called in to break up the crowd).

But we can now reveal where that bash of the year was held — not in London at all, but down in Ronan's local pub in Swords, The Lord Mayor. Of course, by the time our local hero arrived, the word was out and the lower ground floor of the pub was packed, not just with friends and family but with dedicated fans. Some of the more persuasive talkers had managed to charm their way inside! But most remained outside just hoping for a glimpse of the birthday boy.

Ronan's mum, Maria, admitted that although she was very proud of her son and everything he'd achieved, she missed him dreadfully whenever the band headed off on tour. "Ronan is the best, he's a wonderful boy, but I worry about him all the time, especially when he's off travelling so much. He's still so young — they all are and I think people forget that."

But Ronan himself was busy talking about the Summer Tour, and hoping there might be a second Wembley date. Little did he know then that, instead of playing at Wembley Arena once, Boyzone would be playing four sell-out dates! Or was that what he wished for when he blew out those birthday candles?

SHANE
takes the longer look

There were more than a few gasps of amazement when Shane emerged with his new "look" on the second leg of the Summer Tour of '96. Gone were the trademark short, sharp, back and sides, in their place a dark mane suddenly appeared ...

The fashion-conscious Mr Lynch had plumped for hair extentions ("for a bit of a change") which he had attached at a swish London hair salon on 3 July — just two days before the band kicked off on the second leg of their Summer Tour of '96. It was also, coincidentally, the same day the Boyz were due for a photo shoot — who says it's only women who have bad hair days, eh?

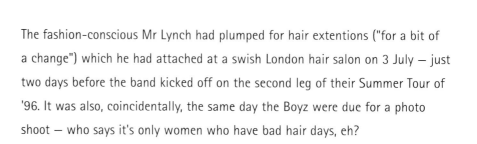

KEITH
father and son

Keith's best moment in '96 had to be the birth of his son Jordan in April. As he says himself, "Becoming a dad is the most amazing experience — though, trying to get all the time I need to spend with Jordan is a problem. Since he's been born though, I've brought him on tour with me for two weeks so I've managed to see quite a lot of him. Looking back, I think I probably feel especially strongly about Jordan because I was very close to everything that went on when Lisa was in labour — for what seemed like ten years!"

The other dad in the band, Mikey, says there are days when he's totally cool with being a dad and days when he just can't get his head around "this whole miracle of life thing". How does Keith feel about the responsibility of being a dad? "It's very scary, suddenly you're looking at this little bundle and you feel so protective and responsible and you've got so much love for him. Then he's kicking and he needs you for every little thing. Suddenly out of the blue you're worried about everything!"

Keith always said that being one of the Boyz was his first priority, but does that mean he can't be there when Jordan needs him? "Absolutely not. I'll always be there for my family and if, God forbid, anything did go wrong with the band, we're well prepared. We've got a lot of good people, friends and family, to take care of us. And, I know your kid's first couple of years are extra-special, but I can't wait for Jordan to get a bit bigger and bolder — then we can have some serious fun together!"

MIKEY
the biker

While everyone else was racing around backstage at Wembley and soaking up the sunshine, Mikey was lost in a world of his own on a vintage Yamaha — which he refused to come down off.

The machine in question belonged to the Boyz' agent, Louis Parker, and once Mikey set his eyes on it he was unstoppable. Decked out in his black leathers he spent the afternoon with a big grin on his face, screeching around between the trucks and spacewagons outside the arena (in a closed off area — much to the disappointment of fans desperate for a better view) giving everyone who'd risk it, the benefit of his biker skills.

S T E V E
goes solo with "if you were mine"

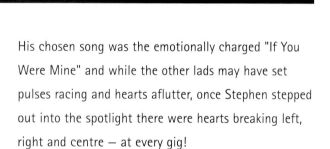

The Summer Tour of '96 was extra special for one Boyzone member in particular — for the first time, Steve got a chance to sing solo and, as far as he and and crowd were concerned, it was a dream come true ...

His chosen song was the emotionally charged "If You Were Mine" and while the other lads may have set pulses racing and hearts aflutter, once Stephen stepped out into the spotlight there were hearts breaking left, right and centre — at every gig!

"It was a brilliant opportunity for me," he said. "I've always wanted to sing solo and it's been great — especially since the fans seem to love it so much. I only have one other dream now and that's to sing on a Disney sound track — then I'll be completely happy!"

Meet

The Boyz love to get out and about to meet their loyal fans. We snapped them doing just that — swapping jokes and signing anything from birthday cards to elbows! Like Keith says, "We're well aware that we've got the best fans — a lot of them are good friends at this stage." The feeling is mutual, as one fan said, "Other popstars don't even acknowledge you but Boyzone spend time getting to know you."

and · Greet

But a word of warning, according to Stephen, some fans just expect too much! "I mean, I'll sign anything for anyone — but some girls just want everything signed ... I just love it when they have some respect for you and say 'thank you' and 'I'm sorry for bothering you' — those fans are great." Stephen takes his fans

very seriously and spends time, even when he's not on tour, signing and sending all sorts of things back to them. "Even when I go home to see my parents, I still sign loads of birthday cards and postcards for fans. I guess I just love to see happiness. I'm one of those people who believes it's important to smile — a lot!"

Highest-Lights

Yes, Boyzone have hit international fame fast and learnt a lot very quickly. But they haven't lost the special qualities that make them such nice guyz — that crazy sense of humour of Shane and Keith's, for example! "Initially my biggest concern was to get them to be more passionate," Ray Hedges, the Boyz' producer on *Said and Done*, remarked. "They were definitely passionate about being successful, but they really needed that to come across when they were performing — somehow, though, listening to them now I don't think that's a problem anymore ..." Somehow, just looking at these pix, we don't think so either! Here's to Boyzone and many more years of fame!

the pictures

KYRAN O'BRIEN is a staff photographer with the *Evening Herald*. Perhaps the best-known shot of his award-winning photography was that world exclusive engagement snap of Naomi Campbell and Adam Clayton back in '92. Kyran's work has appeared worldwide in *Q* magazine, *Rolling Stone*, *The New York Times*, *Hello!* and International Music Magazines, and he's well-known as the rock 'n' roll snapper responsible for all those shots of the rock fraternity. "When Louis Walsh first suggested to me that I photograph the Boyz back when they were just starting out, I thought the whole idea was crazy. However, hundreds of rolls of film later I've well and truly eaten my words. It was their meteoric rise to fame that made me realise I just had to do a book — that and the fact that I had to decide who was more important in my life, Boyzone or my wife Sandra. The shots had to go ...

"But it was Sylvie Redmond who inspired me to give all the proceeds from *Oh Boyz!* to Our Lady's Hospital for Sick Children, Crumlin. Her courage for life in spite of the fact that she was such a sick girl really impressed me an awful lot."

**Photo by
Bryan O'Brien**

the wordz

AILEEN C O'REILLY works for the *Evening Herald* where she writes The Rap daily music column. She has interviewed many international rock greats including REM, Blur, The Cure, The Cranberries, Eternal, Michelle Gayle, Michael Jackson's nephews 3T — and Keanu Reeves ... She's also well-known for having kept tabs on Boyzone ever since Louis Walsh first launched them two years ago. "What interested me most about writing this book was the fact that Boyzone were really the pioneers of Ireland's new pop culture. Suddenly these five Dublin boys, who all the critics dismissed as a five-minute wonder, were on the cover of every teen magazine ... and were being played off the airwaves. It set a precedent for Ireland's music industry. Even the cynics had to admit that this was one bubble that wasn't going to burst. It was just going to get bigger. It did, and now, in the space of two years, we're looking at a new Take That.

"All the royalties raised from this book are going to Our Lady's Hospital for Sick Children — apart from the fact that the hospital is such a worthy cause, I'm sure Boyzone are delighted that a book about them should help any of their fans who might be in that hospital."

© Colm Henry

acknowledgements

This book is not a sole effort by any means. Thanks must be showered on the many people involved ... THANKS to everybody!!

A great deal of people helped to make this book possible. Most importantly, the boys from the band, Ronan, Keith, Shane, Mikey and Stevie who gave me all the access that I needed. The writing of the book was taken on by my colleague Aileen Catherine O'Reilly to whom I am most grateful. She also gave of her time and vast skills for free. I also wish to thank the management of the band, Louis, John, Mark, the people organisers Steve and Barry, Declan Rush from Fuji for all the great film and cameras, Nicola Watkins from CityJet for the first class flights, Cidona for the few bob to pay the bills, Nuala Buttner in Gilmore Communications, my boss Liam Mulcahy and editor Paul Drury in the *Evening Herald* for time off to cover the band, staff at Slattery's Camera Shop, O'Connell Street, all the staff of Photocare Abbey Street for the quick prints, best in Dublin, Jim O'Kelly for the beautiful clean darkroom, Maxwells Picture Agency, Jim Walpole for the fisheye, Sharon and Paul and the staff of Polygram Ireland, Jocelyn in Polydor Paris, the staff of O'Brien Press who could not have been more helpful, also Eamonn Coughlan of Our Lady's Hospital for Sick Children, and Nicky and Martin Smith.

But most of all, my greatest thanks goes to my friend and wife Sandra who has had to put up with me and Boyzone for the duration of this project.

To one and all, thanks a million!

Kyran O'Brien